I0024760

The Role of Local Government in Economic Development

Survey Findings from North Carolina

Jonathan Q. Morgan

June 2009

UNC | SCHOOL OF GOVERNMENT

The School of Government at the University of North Carolina at Chapel Hill works to improve the lives of North Carolinians by engaging in practical scholarship that helps public officials and citizens understand and improve state and local government. Established in 1931 as the Institute of Government, the School provides educational, advisory, and research services for state and local governments. The School of Government is also home to a nationally ranked graduate program in public administration and specialized centers focused on information technology, environmental finance, and civic education for youth.

As the largest university-based local government training, advisory, and research organization in the United States, the School of Government offers up to 200 courses, seminars, and specialized conferences for more than 12,000 public officials each year. In addition, faculty members annually publish approximately fifty books, book chapters, bulletins, and other reference works related to state and local government. Each day that the General Assembly is in session, the School produces the *Daily Bulletin*, which reports on the day's activities for members of the legislature and others who need to follow the course of legislation.

The Master of Public Administration Program is a full-time, two-year program that serves up to sixty students annually. It consistently ranks among the best public administration graduate programs in the country, particularly in city management. With courses ranging from public policy analysis to ethics and management, the program educates leaders for local, state, and federal governments and nonprofit organizations.

Operating support for the School of Government's programs and activities comes from many sources, including state appropriations, local government membership dues, private contributions, publication sales, course fees, and service contracts. Visit www.sog.unc.edu or call 919.966.5381 for more information on the School's courses, publications, programs, and services.

Michael R. Smith, Dean
Thomas H. Thornburg, Senior Associate Dean
Frayda S. Bluestein, Associate Dean for Programs
Todd A. Nicolet, Associate Dean for Operations
Ann Cary Simpson, Associate Dean for Development and Communications
Bradley G. Volk, Associate Dean for Administration

Faculty

Gregory S. Allison
David N. Ammons
Ann M. Anderson
A. Fleming Bell, II
Maureen M. Berner
Mark F. Botts
Joan G. Brannon
Michael Crowell
Shea Riggsbee Denning
James C. Drennan
Richard D. Ducker
Robert L. Farb
Joseph S. Ferrell
Alyson A. Grine
Milton S. Heath Jr.
Norma Houston (on leave)
Cheryl Daniels Howell
Jeffrey A. Hughes

Joseph E. Hunt
Willow S. Jacobson
Robert P. Joyce
Kenneth L. Joyner
Diane M. Juffras
David M. Lawrence
Dona G. Lewandowski
James M. Markham
Janet Mason
Laurie L. Mesibov
Christopher B. McLaughlin
Kara A. Millonzi
Jill D. Moore
Jonathan Q. Morgan
Ricardo S. Morse
C. Tyler Mulligan
David W. Owens
William C. Rivenbark

Dale J. Roenigk
John Rubin
John L. Saxon
Jessica Smith
Karl W. Smith
Carl W. Stenberg III
John B. Stephens
Charles A. Szypszak
Shannon H. Tufts
Vaughn Upshaw
A. John Vogt
Aimee N. Wall
Jeffrey B. Welty
Richard B. Whisnant
Gordon P. Whitaker
Eileen R. Youens

© 2009
School of Government
The University of North Carolina at Chapel Hill

Use of this publication for commercial purposes or without acknowledgment of its source is prohibited. Reproducing, distributing, or otherwise making available to a non-purchaser the entire publication, or a substantial portion of it, without express permission, is prohibited.
Printed in the United States of America
13 12 11 10 09   3 4 5 6 7
ISBN 978-1-56011-612-7

Contents

The Role of Local Government in Economic Development

Survey Findings from North Carolina

Jonathan Q. Morgan

Introduction

The current economic downturn provides a useful context for taking stock of what local governments in North Carolina are doing to stimulate private investment and job creation. The forthcoming federal stimulus funds will only bolster the ongoing efforts of localities to bring about economic development. This report discusses the findings from a mail survey of local government economic development activities that was sent to all 540 municipalities and 100 counties in North Carolina. An important part of the analysis examines whether cities and counties differ significantly in their economic development efforts and whether the size of a jurisdiction is related to the types of development strategies and tools utilized by a local government.

The role of local government in the process of economic development has been extensively studied. Much of the previous research has focused on larger, urban jurisdictions. We therefore know very little about what smaller cities, towns, and counties are doing to promote economic development. Thus it is useful to study North Carolina because it is made up mostly of small local jurisdictions. The data presented in this report will help local officials within the state better understand what strategies and tools are available for achieving economic development in their respective jurisdictions. The report first briefly reviews what we know from previous research on local government economic development activities. It then describes the survey protocol and presents and interprets key findings. The final section offers some concluding thoughts and implications.

What Local Governments Do in Economic Development

There is a vast amount of existing research on the economic development activities of local governments.[1] Early studies sought to identify the most common types of policy tools adopted and used by cities and counties. More recently, the economic development survey conducted every five years by the International City/County Management Association (ICMA) has shed light on what local governments throughout the nation are doing to spur private investment and job creation.[2] However, the ICMA survey data for North Carolina do not adequately capture the efforts of smaller-sized jurisdictions.[3] While some researchers have collected their own survey data for the entire United States or for a particular state or region[4], no separate published survey of local economic development activities in North Carolina exists.

---

1. For a comprehensive review of the literature on local economic development policy, see Harold Wolman and David Spitzley, "The Politics of Local Economic Development," *Economic Development Quarterly* 10 (1996):115–50; or Laura A. Reese and Raymond A. Rosenfeld, *The Civic Culture of Economic Development* (Thousand Oaks, CA: Sage Publications, 2002).

2. For an analysis of the 2004 data collected by International City/County Management Association (ICMA), see Stephen G. Koven and Thomas S. Lyons, "Economic Development: What Local Governments Do," *ICMA Special Data Issue* 2 (2005): 1–12.

3. North Carolina local governments are significantly underrepresented in the 2004 ICMA Economic Development Survey data, which includes only 26 cities and counties.

4. For example, see Herbert J. Rubin, "Local Economic Development Organizations and the Activities of Small Cities in Encouraging Economic Growth," *Policy Studies Journal* 14 (1986): 363–89; John P. Pelissero and David Fasenfest, "A Typology of Suburban Economic Development Policy Orientations," *Economic Development Quarterly* 3 (1989): 301–11; Laura A. Reese, "Local Economic Development in Michigan: A Reliance on the Supply Side," *Economic Development Quarterly* 6 (1992): 383–93;

Irrespective of the source of the data, the most frequently cited local development activities in previous studies include regulations, infrastructure investments, marketing, and tax incentives. Local governments most often use regulatory tools such as zoning and permit assistance and infrastructure upgrades like street improvements and water and sewer extensions.[5] Marketing and promotion activities such as site inventories and brochures are also widely used.[6] Previous research indicates that tax abatements and tax increment financing are the most common tax incentives that local governments utilize for economic development.[7]

Some analysts claim that local governments are moving beyond the traditional activities associated with industrial recruitment and gravitating toward alternative approaches like business retention and entrepreneurship development.[8] Another aspect of this apparent shift in strategy is the emergence of a distinct set of development policies that serve the broader public interest, benefit disadvantaged communities or minorities, and ensure accountability. These so-called Type II policies seek a more equitable distribution of economic development costs and benefits and may include impact fees, requirements for hiring local residents or using minority-owned firms, provision of low-income housing, and business performance guarantees.[9] It remains to be seen whether these approaches represent a wholesale paradigm shift in economic development. The survey data reported below will show the

extent to which North Carolina local governments are part of this wave of economic development change.[10]

Unresolved Questions

What Makes North Carolina Different?

One problem with the existing research on local government economic development activities is that it fails to account for differences in enabling legislation and legal frameworks across states. For example, tax abatements are the most commonly studied economic development incentive at the local level, but several states do not allow local governments to outright abate taxes. In North Carolina, local tax abatements violate the state constitution.[11] While 48 other states have used tax increment financing extensively for many years, North Carolina did not authorize its use until 2004, when voters passed an amendment to the state constitution. Although one prior study explicitly examines the effects of state laws that prohibit local property tax abatements, the ICMA data it used had a low response rate from local governments in North Carolina.[12] It will be helpful to know what local governments do to achieve economic development in a state like North Carolina, where options are constrained by legal and constitutional considerations.

Does Population Size Matter?

There is good reason to think that the size of the population in a jurisdiction will influence its approach to economic development. However, the limited data available on the development activities of small towns makes it difficult to know for sure. Many qualitative case studies and stories of small town success exist,[13] but quantitative research on what small towns do in terms of economic development is scant. The ICMA economic development survey and the vast majority of quantitative studies focus on larger cities; that is, cities with populations

---

Laura A. Reese, "Local Economic Development Practices Across the Northern Border, *Urban Affairs Quarterly* 28 (1993): 571–92.

5. Thomas S. Lyons and Steven G. Koven, "Economic Development and Public Policy at the Local Government Level," *ICMA Municipal Year Book* (2006): 11–18; Laura A. Reese and Raymond A. Rosenfeld, "Local Economic Development in the United States and Canada: Institutionalizing Policy Approaches," *American Review of Public Administration* 34 (2004): 277–92; Daniel M. Sullivan, "Local Governments as Risk Takers and Risk Reducers: An Examination of Business Subsidies and Subsidy Controls," *Economic Development Quarterly* 16 (2002): 115–26.

6. Laura A. Reese and David Fasenfest, "More of the Same: A Research Note on Local Economic Development Policies Over Time," *Economic Development Quarterly* 10 (1996): 280–89.

7. The precise ranking of specific activities and tools varies across studies. For examples, see Stephen G. Koven and Thomas S. Lyons, "Economic Development: What Local Governments Do, *ICMA Special Data Issue* 2 (2005): 1–12 ; Laura A. Reese, "Local Economic Development in Michigan: A Reliance on the Supply Side, *Economic Development Quarterly* 6 (1992): 383–393; Daniel M. Sullivan, "Local Governments as Risk Takers and Risk Reducers: An Examination of Business Subsidies and Subsidy Controls, *Economic Development Quarterly* 16 (2002): 115–26.

8. Peter K. Eisinger, *The Rise of the Entrepreneurial State*, (Madison, WI: University of Wisconsin Press, 1988); Susan E. Clarke and Gary L. Gaile, "The Next Wave: Postfederal Local Economic Development Strategies, *Economic Development Quarterly* 6 (1992): 187–98.

9. Edward G. Goetz, "Type II Policy and Mandated Benefits in Economic Development, *Urban Affairs Quarterly* 26 (1990): 170–90; David R. Elkins, "Testing Competing Explanations for the Adoption of Type II Policies," *Urban Affairs Review* 30 (1995): 809–39; Laura A. Reese, "Sharing the Benefits of Economic Development: What Cities Use Type II Policies?" *Urban Affairs Review* 33 (1998): 686–711; Carla Jean Robinson, "Municipal Approaches to Economic Development: Growth and Distribution Policy, *Journal of the American Planning Association* 55 (1989): 283–94.

10. The wave metaphor has been used to describe the evolution of economic development policy from a primary emphasis on industrial recruitment (e.g., "smokestack chasing") in the first wave to so-called second-wave business retention and entrepreneurship strategies. Most recently it has been applied to so-called third-wave principles that require new governance and implementation techniques. See Ted K. Bradshaw and Edward J. Blakely, "What Are "Third Wave" State Economic Development Efforts? From Incentives to Industrial Policy," *Economic Development Quarterly* 13 (1999): 229–44; Doug Ross and Robert E. Friedman, "The Emerging Third Wave: New Economic Development Strategies in the '90s," *The Entrepreneurial Economy Review* 9 (1990): 3–10.

11. David M. Lawrence, *Economic Development Law for North Carolina Local Governments* (Chapel Hill, NC: UNC Institute of Government, 2000).

12. Laura A. Reese and Amy B. Malmer, "The Effects of State Enabling Legislation on Local Economic Development Policies," *Urban Affairs Quarterly* 30 (1994): 114–35. The authors used data for cities from the 1989 ICMA Economic Development Survey, which included only 16 North Carolina municipalities.

13. For example, see Will Lambe, *Small Towns, Big Ideas: Case Studies in Small Town Community Economic Development* (Chapel Hill, NC: UNC School of Government and NC Rural Economic Development Center, 2008.), available at www.cednc.unc.edu/stbi.

exceeding 10,000. The existing research does not adequately reflect what might be occurring in states that are made up mainly of smaller jurisdictions. For example, of the 548 municipalities in North Carolina, 480, or 87 percent, have populations of less than 10,000. To address this gap, most of the data presented in this report are separated out for jurisdictions with fewer than 10,000 residents.

It is expected that smaller jurisdictions will employ fewer economic development tools overall due to resource and capacity constraints. Being a small jurisdiction can have some drawbacks, but it can also create conditions that necessitate innovation. The high cost, uncertainty, and uneven results of traditional industrial recruitment might cause smaller communities to experiment with promising alternative strategies such as business retention and entrepreneurship development. Despite their doing less overall, it is reasonable to think that smaller communities might prefer an approach to economic development that is qualitatively different than that of larger jurisdictions. The survey data discussed in this report will show whether or not this proves true for small jurisdictions in North Carolina.

Do Counties Play a Special Role?

Some researchers believe that there is a specialization of roles between cities and counties with respect to economic development. This viewpoint suggests that counties are inclined to fulfill a regional coordinating function for towns and municipalities and emphasize different types of economic development activities.[14] In their regional coordinating role, counties are expected to focus on longer-range goals, to be more active in strategic planning and program evaluation, and to be more inclined to collaborate and to engage a larger number of partner organizations.

There is some tentative evidence that, in addition to providing strategic regional leadership, counties tend to employ alternative economic development tools—such as small business incubators, export assistance, and job training—to a greater extent than cities.[15] Compared to industrial recruitment, these ostensibly more innovative approaches to economic development do not typically produce highly visible, short-term benefits, and thus they require the longer-term view that counties purportedly take. For example, investing in quality-of-life amenities to promote economic development necessitates the sort of patience and persistence that counties seem well suited to demonstrate. Moreover, it can be argued that counties generally have access to more resources and greater capacity to promote private investment, which makes it easier for them to expand their economic development

activities to include more innovative policy tools. The results reported below will reveal the extent to which North Carolina counties play this distinctive role in the process of economic development.

The Survey of Local Government Economic Development Activities

The data analyzed in this study come from a mail survey conducted in late 2005 and early 2006. Questionnaires were mailed to chief administrators in all 648 local governments (548 municipalities and 100 counties) in North Carolina. In many cases, the chief administrator forwarded the questionnaire to the person responsible for economic development in the jurisdiction. A total of 217 useable surveys were returned for an overall response rate of 33 percent, which is respectable for mail surveys of this type.[16] Responses came from 150, or 27 percent, of the municipalities and 67 of the 100 counties in the state (see Table 1). The percentage of respondents from jurisdictions with less than 10,000 in population (50.7) is roughly equal to the percentage of those with 10,000 or more in population (49.3). Of the municipalities that responded to the survey, 72 percent have less than 10,000 in population, compared to only 3 percent of counties. Municipalities comprise 98 percent of the responding jurisdictions smaller than 10,000.

The next section reports the responses to selected survey questions. The percentages of respondents are reported for the entire sample of local governments and also by jurisdiction type (city or county) and population size (less than 10,000, and 10,000 and higher). Some questions required respondents to indicate on a five-point scale a particular level of participation in selected activities or their agreement with certain statements. The mean (average) scores are reported for the responses to these questions.

Survey Results

Overview

The data in Table 2 provide a snapshot of the capacity for and the extent of economic development activities among local governments in North Carolina. There are clear differences between cities and counties and between smaller and larger jurisdictions. The average number of full-time economic development staff positions is less than one (0.859) across all local governments responding to the survey. The break out by type of jurisdiction shows that cities on average devote just more than half of a full-time equivalent to economic development, while counties employ slightly more than 1.5 staff positions in this function. Smaller jurisdictions have much less staff capacity for economic development, with an average of only 0.16 of a

14. Linda Lobao and David S. Kraybill, "The Emerging Roles of County Governments in Metropolitan and Nonmetropolitan Areas: Findings from a National Survey," *Economic Development Quarterly* 19 (2005): 245–59; Laura A. Reese, "The Role of Counties in Local Economic Development," *Economic Development Quarterly* 8 (1994): 28–42.

15. Laura A. Reese, "The Role of Counties in Local Economic Development," *Economic Development Quarterly* 8 (1994): 28–42.

16. For example, the response rate for the 2004 ICMA Economic Development Survey was 19.6 percent.

**Table 1. Survey Respondents
by Population and Jurisdiction Type**

	Number Responding		
Population	All	Cities	Counties
Less than 10,000	110	108	2
10,000–24,999	35	24	11
25,000–74,999	40	9	31
75,000–124,999	11	3	8
125,000–199,999	12	2	10
200,000+	9	4	5
n	217	150	67

**Table 2. Summary Data on Economic
Development Capacity and Effort (Mean Score)**

				Population	
	All	Cities	Counties	<10,000	≥10,000
ED staff	0.859	0.559	1.574	0.160	1.600
Organizational participant index	7.203	5.713	10.537	4.746	9.729
Index of total ED effort	8.677	6.273	14.060	4.482	12.991
Recruitment index	5.857	4.300	9.343	3.282	8.505
Retention index	2.912	1.973	5.015	1.518	4.346
Small business index	1.230	0.773	2.254	0.500	1.981

**Table 3. Primary Focus of Economic
Development Efforts (Percent Reporting)**

				Population	
	All	Cities	Counties	<10,000	≥10,000
Manufacturing	41.5	32.0	62.7	25.5	57.9
Tourism/hospitality	21.7	22.0	20.9	23.6	19.6
Retail/service	19.4	22.0	13.4	23.6	15.0
High tech industries	17.1	12.7	26.9	8.2	26.2
Warehousing/distribution	10.6	7.3	17.9	6.4	15.0
Residential	8.8	10.0	6.0	12.7	4.7
Retirement community	7.8	7.3	9.0	6.4	9.3
Other	7.8	5.3	13.4	2.7	13.1
Institutional	5.5	6.0	4.5	5.5	5.6
Agricultural	4.1	4.0	4.5	5.5	2.8
n	217	150	67	110	107

full-time position. The low levels of internal staff available to work on economic development in small jurisdictions might make it more difficult to engage with other organizations. This is evident in the mean scores on the index of organizational participants, which count the total number of partner groups involved in a jurisdiction's economic development efforts.

The range of organizations involved in economic development efforts varies based on jurisdiction type and size (see Table 2). (Specific types of organizations are reported later in the discussion.) The average number of organizations participating in city activities is 5.71, which is nearly half that of counties at 10.54 (out of a possible 18). Smaller jurisdictions have an average of 4.75 organizations engaged in their economic development efforts, while larger communities use 9.73 organizations on average. As an indicator of local capacity for economic development, the mean scores on the organizational participant index point to an advantage for counties and larger jurisdictions. These findings may also provide some initial evidence that counties, in particular, serve a regional coordinating role in economic development.

The other indexes shown in Table 2 reflect the sum count of economic development activities indicated by respondents. According to the index of total effort, local governments in

North Carolina use an average of 8.68 different tools and techniques (out of a possible 30) for economic development. (Specific tools and activities are reported later in the discussion.) The highest number of activities support business recruitment (5.86), while significantly fewer small business development tools are used (1.23). Counties engage in a much larger array of activities than do cities. The mean scores on the composite indexes vary considerably by both jurisdiction type and population size. These results confirm that larger jurisdictions have a broader portfolio of economic development activities and tools than smaller communities.

The emphasis on business recruitment activities is likely related to the targeting of manufacturing that is apparent among jurisdictions. As shown in Table 3, the highest percentage of respondents across all categories (city, county, and population size) indicated that manufacturing is the primary focus of local government economic development efforts. The order of the next most common target industries differs slightly among cities, counties, and smaller communities. For cities, manufacturing is followed by tourism, retail/services, high tech industries, and residential. After manufacturing, counties tend to focus more on high tech industries, tourism, warehousing/distribution, and retail/services. By contrast, the preference of smaller communities is more evenly distributed and concentrated on manufacturing, tourism, and retail/services. Residential development and high tech industries round out the top five areas of focus for smaller jurisdictions.

Over the past decade, many North Carolina jurisdictions have seen a steady influx of new residents and have experienced strong growth in the residential building sector of the local economy. While growth in population and residential develop-

Table 4. Composition of Tax Base in Jurisdiction (Percent Reporting)

	All	Cities	Counties	Population <10,000	Population ≥10,000
Mostly residential	52.1	60.0	34.3	70.9	32.7
Mostly retail/ commercial	3.7	4.7	1.5	3.6	3.7
Mostly industrial	0.9	1.3	0.0	0.9	0.9
Diverse mix	41.9	32.7	62.7	21.8	62.6
n	217	150	67	110	107

Table 5. Economic Development Tools by Strategy (Percent Reporting)

Business Recruitment

Responding to prospect inquiries	68.7
Regional partnership	65.4
Partnership with chamber	59.4
Website/community profile	57.1
Building and sites inventory	42.4
Provide high quality of life	41.9
Cash grant incentives	41.5

Business Retention and Expansion

Existing industry calls and visits	48.4
Buiness networking	30.9
Cash grant incentives	29.0
Partnering with other local gov'ts	28.6
Worker training assistance	28.6
Partnering with nongov't entities	28.6
Surveys of local businesses	24.9

Entrepreneurship and Business Creation

Small business development center	27.2
Business incubator	15.7
Marketing assistance	15.7
Revolving loan fund	14.7
Property improvement grants	11.5
Other	11.1
Microenterprise program	9.2
n	217

ment are important sources of economic activity, they also create costs for local government and increase the demand for public services such as water/sewer, schools, and law enforcement. An increasing number of jurisdictions rely on a local tax base comprised mostly of residential property. In general, residential development does not generate sufficient tax revenues to pay for the costs of public services it requires.[17] By contrast, commercial and industrial development usually pays for itself and produces net tax revenue in excess of the costs for public services. The challenge for "bedroom communities," whose residents commute to work in another jurisdiction, is figuring out how to get a more diversified employment and tax base. Table 4 shows that this may be a particularly acute problem for smaller towns responding to the survey, as 71 percent of them describe their tax base as mostly residential.

Economic Development Strategies and Tools

The individual activities and tools used to support broad economic development strategies are shown in Table 5. The data indicate that local governments in North Carolina are much more likely to engage in various activities to recruit new firms than they are to use specific mechanisms to retain existing firms or create their own. While local governments frequently respond directly to inquiries from prospective businesses, it is clear that they rely on other entities, such as regional partnership organizations and chambers of commerce, to help with business recruitment. Local governments frequently use information and data tools, such as Web-based community profiles and building/sites inventories, to support business recruitment. Providing a high quality of life and cash grant incentives are also important business recruitment tools for the jurisdictions participating in the survey.

Although local governments in North Carolina seem to prefer business recruitment activities, they are also active in retention and business creation. The top business retention activity is existing industry calls and visitation, followed by business networking. Less than a third of respondents indicated that cash incentives are used to retain and expand existing companies. A higher percentage of local governments

use cash incentive grants for recruitment rather than for retention/expansion, despite the fact that existing companies are more dependable sources of new jobs and investment.[18] Less than a third of responding local governments partner with other local governments or nongovernmental entities on business retention activities. Much lower percentages of the responding jurisdictions reported using specific entrepreneurship and business creation tools. The highest percentage indicated that they defer to small business development centers to help support the start-up and growth of new firms. The small number of local governments that directly support entrepreneurship and small business development tend to use business incubators, marketing assistance, revolving loan funds, and property improvement (facade) grants. Eleven percent of respondents reported using some other tool for small business development that was not listed on the survey

17. Timothy W. Kelsey, "The Fiscal Impacts of Alternative Land Uses: What Do Cost of Community Service Studies Really Tell Us?" *Journal of the Community Development Society* 27 (1996): 78–90.

18. Henry M. Cothran, "Business Retention and Expansion (BRE) Programs: Why Existing Business are Important" (University of Florida, IFAS Extension, 2009), available at http://edis.ifas.ufl.edu/pdffiles/FE/FE65100.pdf (accessed April 24, 2009).

Table 6. Economic Development Tools (Percent Reporting)

	All	Cities	Counties	Population <10,000	Population ≥10,000
Zoning and permit assistance	59.0	59.3	58.2	57.3	60.7
Infrastructure improvements	56.2	49.3	71.6	40.0	72.9
Cash grant incentives	42.4	28.7	73.1	15.5	70.1
One-stop permitting	30.0	22.7	46.3	16.4	43.9
State development zone	24.0	19.3	34.3	5.5	43.0
Land or building acquisition	23.0	12.7	46.3	7.3	39.3
Site preparation	19.4	10.7	38.8	6.4	32.7
Subsidized land or buildings	17.5	12.0	29.9	7.3	28.0
Subsidized worker training	16.1	6.0	38.8	2.7	29.9
Tax increment financing	15.7	10.0	28.4	2.7	29.0
Low-interest loans	11.1	8.7	16.4	0.9	21.5
Relocation assistance	9.2	3.3	22.4	2.7	15.9
Employee screening	9.2	1.3	26.9	0.0	18.7
Regulatory flexibility	7.8	5.3	13.4	0.9	15.0
Incentives for retail projects	7.4	4.0	14.9	2.7	12.1
Private utility rate reduction	6.0	3.3	11.9	1.8	10.3
n	217	150	67	110	107

Table 7. Level of Participation in Selected Activities

	All	Cities	Counties	Population <10,000	Population ≥10,000
Workforce development/ job training	2.26	1.66	3.38	1.62	2.78
Industrial parks operated by local government	2.25	1.92	2.87	1.77	2.65
Community development corporation	2.05	1.84	2.46	1.56	2.48
Land banking and assembly	1.71	1.54	2.05	1.27	2.09
Construction and marketing of shell buildings	1.64	1.39	2.13	1.35	1.89
Local government sponsored loan program	1.47	1.40	1.61	1.19	1.70
Equity financing for private firms	1.13	1.08	1.23	1.05	1.19

Note: Mean score on a 5-point scale

questionnaire. These included incentive grants and technical assistance.

Incentives by Jurisdiction Type and Population Size

Irrespective of broad strategy (recruitment, retention, and entrepreneurship), the most frequently used economic development tools overall are zoning and permit assistance, infrastructure improvements, cash grant incentives, and streamlined "one-stop" permitting (see Table 6). However, the exact order of preferences differs slightly based on jurisdiction type and population size. The ranking of commonly used tools and incentives for cities closely resembles that of the total sample. The highest percentage of counties reported using cash grant incentives (73.1 percent), followed by infrastructure improvements (71.6 percent) and zoning and permit assistance (58.2 percent). The break out of incentives by population size shows the same tools among the top four.

The most obvious finding in Table 6 is that much higher percentages of both counties and larger jurisdictions use the various economic development tools and incentives. Except for zoning and permit assistance, there are significant differences between cities and counties and between smaller and larger jurisdictions in the use of nearly every type of incentive. In particular, counties are much more likely than cities to provide cash incentive grants, subsidize the cost of worker training, assist with employee screening, and assist with land or building acquisition and site preparation. Compared to smaller communities, significantly higher percentages of the larger jurisdictions reported using these same incentives along with state development zones, tax increment financing, and low interest loans. Larger cities and counties are more likely to have pockets of urban blight that might benefit from geographic targeting of resources and expanded financing mechanisms.

When asked about the level of participation in selected economic development activities, survey respondents could select a value ranging from one (very low) to five (very high). The results in Table 7 show relatively moderate to low levels of participation overall in the selected activities. Counties and larger jurisdictions participate in workforce development, industrial parks, community development corporations, shell building construction, and land banking/assembly to a greater extent than cities and small communities. Local governments in North Carolina are only minimally involved in providing debt and equity financing to companies.

Table 8. Quality of Life Investments as Economic Development (Percent Reporting)

	All	Cities	Counties	Population <10,000	Population ≥10,000
Public parks	62.2	64.0	58.2	60.9	63.6
Public safety	53.9	56.0	49.3	50.0	57.9
Tourism development	52.5	42.7	74.6	38.2	67.3
Downtown development	47.9	48.7	46.3	35.5	60.7
Historic preservation	42.9	40.7	47.8	32.7	53.3
Local libraries	39.2	32.0	55.2	29.1	49.5
Local schools/ public education	38.2	26.0	65.7	30.0	46.7
Development of local arts	30.4	26.7	38.8	15.5	45.8
Amateur sports/ recreation complex	28.6	26.0	34.3	17.3	40.2
Affordable housing	25.3	26.7	22.4	16.4	34.6
Theater/arts center	22.6	21.3	25.4	11.8	33.6
Transportation/ mass transit	22.1	18.0	31.3	5.5	39.3
Medical/health care facilities	19.8	14.0	32.8	13.6	26.2
Convention center	11.5	10.0	14.9	3.6	19.6
Child care	6.5	4.0	11.9	1.8	11.2
n	217	150	67	110	107

Quality of Life as Economic Development

Quality of life has become an increasingly important source of competitive advantage for communities seeking to stimulate private investment in a global economy. Companies that employ highly educated and skilled workers care about quality of life issues in large part because their workers prefer to live in places with amenities such as good schools, parks, walking trails, cultural activities and the like.[19] As noted above, 42 percent of local governments in North Carolina consider their investments in quality of life to be a tool for recruiting new businesses. But what specific types of quality of life investments are most widely used for economic development? Table 8 shows the survey responses to this question.

Overall, investing in public parks is the preferred quality of life tool for economic development. This is followed by public safety, tourism development, downtown development, and historic preservation. Cities indicated a similar pattern in their use of these specific quality of life investments to promote economic development. However, the highest percentages of counties indicated that they invest in tourism development (74.6 percent) and public schools[20] (65.7 percent) as quality of life levers for stimulating economic activity. Counties are also much more likely than cities to invest in public libraries, sports and recreation complexes, and medical/health care facilities in support of economic development. Compared to smaller communities, larger jurisdictions make investments in a much wider array of quality of life activities. Larger local governments differ most significantly in their use of transportation/mass transit, local arts, theaters, tourism, downtown development, sports/recreation complexes, and convention centers.

Goals, Planning, and Accountability

For many years, the practice of economic development, particularly industrial recruitment, was not typically guided by systematic planning and strategic focus. Instead, it was akin to "shooting at anything that flies and claiming anything that falls to the ground."[21] Increased global competition and economic uncertainty have led communities to be more strategic in their approaches to economic development. If this trend is taking hold in North Carolina, there ought to be a wide range of clearly defined goals that local governments use to determine which specific strategies and tools they employ. These goals might logically vary based on jurisdiction type and size. In addition, there should be evidence that jurisdictions are utilizing strategic planning, program evaluation, and other accountability mechanisms. After all, being strategic in economic development is about choosing the strategies and tools that are best suited to a community's goals, using safeguards to protect the public investment, and measuring success (or failure).

The most frequently cited economic development goal among local governments in North Carolina is expanding the tax base (see Table 9). Job creation is a close second, followed by new business recruitment, retention and growth of existing firms, and diversifying the economic base. More than half of the survey respondents indicated that their jurisdiction's goals include providing higher quality jobs (59.9 percent), promoting entrepreneurship (53.9 percent), and attracting retail/services (53.0 percent). The least-cited economic development

19. See Richard Florida, *The Rise of the Creative Class* (New York: Basic Books, 2002); Kilungu Nzaku and James O. Bukenya, "Examining the Relationship between Quality of Life Amenities and Economic Development in the Southeast USA," *Review of Urban and Regional Development Studies* 17 (2005): 89–103; David Salvensen and Henry Renski, *The Importance of Quality of Life in the Location Decisions of New Economy Firms* (Washington, DC: Economic Development

Administration, 2002), available at www.eda.gov/PDF/UNC_Lit_Rev1.pdf.

20. Cities in North Carolina do not fund public school systems, but counties share the costs of public schools with the state.

21. Hebert J. Rubin, "Shoot Anything That Flies; Claim Anything That Falls: Conversations with Economic Development Practitioners," *Economic Development Quarterly* 2 (1988): 236–51.

Table 9. Goals of Economic Development (Percent Reporting)

	All	Cities	Counties	Population <10,000	Population ≥10,000
Expand tax base	78.8	74.0	89.6	70.0	87.9
Job creation	76.5	68.7	94.0	61.8	91.6
Recruit new business	73.7	65.3	92.5	58.2	89.7
Retain and grow existing business	70.5	62.0	89.6	54.5	86.9
Diversify economic base	63.1	52.0	88.1	44.5	82.2
Higher paying/ better jobs	59.9	47.3	88.1	40.9	79.4
Promote entrepreneurship	53.9	45.3	73.1	42.7	65.4
Attract retail and services	53.0	53.3	52.2	55.5	50.5
Control growth	43.3	46.0	37.3	48.2	38.3
Promote social and economic equity	22.6	20.7	26.9	19.1	26.2
Wealth creation	20.7	13.3	37.3	10.0	31.8
Other	7.8	6.0	11.9	5.5	10.3
n	217	150	67	110	107

Table 10. Planning and Accountability Mechanisms (Percent Reporting)

	All	Cities	Counties	Population <10,000	Population ≥10,000
Has a strategic plan for ED	41.9	32.0	64.2	21.8	62.6
Evaluates ED activities	41.2	30.7	65.2	19.1	64.2
Always require performance agreement	51.2	40.0	76.1	25.5	77.6
Sometimes require performance agreement	14.3	14.7	13.4	17.3	11.2
n	217	150	67	110	107
Clawback provisions	60.7	47.4	86.4	28.2	87.4
Cost–benefit analysis	59.5	48.6	79.0	31.6	81.4
Formal policy for incentives eligibility	51.1	42.6	66.7	28.2	69.0
Hire local residents	18.3	15.9	22.6	12.8	22.7
n	175	114	60	78	95

goals were controlling growth (43.3 percent), promoting equity (22.6 percent), and creating wealth (20.7 percent). Cities and counties differ in their stated preference for specific goals. The highest percentage of cities engage in economic development to expand the tax base, whereas the largest share of counties see job creation as a goal. The goal of attracting retail and service businesses is shared by similar percentages of counties and cities and large and small jurisdictions. It is notable that the percentages of smaller communities concerned about controlling growth and attracting retail and service businesses actually exceed those of larger jurisdictions. It is clear that counties and larger jurisdictions are more likely to pursue a wider range of economic development goals. This may reflect differences in the resources and capacity available for planning and systematically identifying what communities are trying to achieve.

There is great variation in the use of strategic planning and accountability mechanisms among local governments in North Carolina. As shown in Table 10, less than half (42 percent) of local governments have adopted a strategic plan for economic development. However, counties and larger jurisdictions are more likely than cities and smaller communities to have a formal plan. The percentages of local governments that evaluate their economic development efforts follow a very similar pattern, with counties and larger jurisdictions showing a greater tendency to do so. The most common accountability mecha-

nisms are performance-based contracts, clawback provisions,[22] and cost–benefit analysis. Counties are much more likely than cities to use these mechanisms. The same is true for larger jurisdictions as compared to smaller communities. Very few local governments in North Carolina require companies to hire local residents as a condition for receiving incentives.[23]

Slightly more than half of all respondents (51.2 percent) indicated that their local government always requires a written performance agreement when providing incentives to companies. Another 14.3 percent of responding jurisdictions reported that they sometimes require such formal agreements. Much higher percentages of counties and larger jurisdictions mandate performance agreements. Counties and larger jurisdictions are more likely to have a formal policy that specifies the criteria for receiving economic development incentives. Table 11 shows that the preferred incentive criteria are the level of capital

22. Clawbacks are penalty provisions in incentive contracts that require companies to pay back some or all of the incentive monies they received if they fail to meet performance expectations within a certain period.
23. Placing such a condition on receiving incentives might be vulnerable to legal and constitutional challenges. See David Lawrence, *Economic Development Law for North Carolina Local Governments* (Chapel Hill, NC: UNC Institute of Government, 2000).

Table 11. Incentive Criteria Used (Percent Reporting)

	All	Cities	Counties	Population <10,000	≥10,000
Capital investment	57.1	44.0	86.6	30.9	84.1
New jobs created	56.7	46.7	79.1	34.5	79.4
New tax revenue generated	49.3	36.0	79.1	24.5	74.8
Wage levels of new jobs	39.2	26.7	67.2	16.4	62.6
Type of business/ industry	31.8	26.0	44.8	16.4	47.7
Public investment payback	27.2	21.3	40.3	8.2	46.7
Company performance	11.1	7.3	19.4	4.5	17.8
Other	9.2	12.0	3.0	11.8	6.5
n	217	150	67	110	107

investment, number of jobs created, and amount of new tax revenue generated by companies.

Governance and Service Delivery

Local government appears to play a significant role in carrying out economic development activities in North Carolina. Forty-one percent of respondents indicated that a unit of local government has primary responsibility for economic development in their respective jurisdictions. Roughly a quarter of respondents each indicated that either a nonprofit organization is primarily responsible for economic development or no single entity is responsible. A higher percentage of counties (50.7 percent) reported that local government is the entity most responsible for economic development, while nearly a third indicated that a nonprofit group takes the lead. One-third (32.7 percent) of smaller communities reported that no single organization is primarily responsible for economic development in their jurisdiction. The department within a unit of local government that takes the lead on economic development varies across jurisdictions. Cities are more likely to administer economic development through the city/town manager's office, whereas counties prefer to use a separate economic development department.

It was noted above that counties and larger jurisdictions engage a greater number of other organizations in their economic development efforts. It is also useful to know which specific types of organizations are involved in economic development and whether they differ between cities and counties and between smaller and larger communities. These results are shown in Table 12. Overall, the most commonly reported external organizations include chambers of commerce, community colleges, the state commerce department, regional economic development partnership organizations,

Table 12. Organizational Participants in Economic Development (Percent Reporting)

	All	Cities	Counties	Population <10,000	≥10,000
Municipal government	77.0	74.0	83.6	69.1	85.0
County government	76.0	68.7	92.5	64.5	87.9
Chamber of commerce	71.4	67.3	80.6	60.0	83.2
Elected officials	71.4	64.7	86.6	57.3	86.0
Community college	59.0	45.3	89.6	33.6	85.0
State Commerce Department	56.7	43.3	86.6	30.9	83.2
Regional ED partnership	47.5	32.0	82.1	25.5	70.1
Local ED commission	41.5	30.0	67.2	29.1	54.2
Nonprofit EDC	38.7	28.0	62.7	15.5	62.6
Council of Gov't	38.7	32.7	52.2	32.7	44.9
Private utility	36.4	22.0	68.7	15.5	57.9
Local workforce board	23.5	10.0	53.7	4.5	43.0
Citizen advisory board	22.1	14.0	40.3	9.1	35.5
University	18.9	12.0	34.3	9.1	29.0
Community development corporation	18.0	14.0	26.9	8.2	28.0
Federal government	17.1	10.0	32.8	6.4	28.0
Other	6.9	7.3	6.0	9.1	4.7
Industrial development authority	6.5	3.3	13.4	3.6	9.3
n	217	150	67	110	107

and local economic development commissions. The listing of most-common organizational participants for cities and counties is very similar. However, counties are much more likely also to involve private utilities, local workforce development boards, nonprofit economic development corporations, and citizen advisory boards. It is worth noting that the highest percentage of counties, 89.6 percent, indicated that community colleges participate in their economic development efforts, compared to just 45.3 percent of cities.

As shown in Table 13, the most frequently cited source of funding for economic development among responding jurisdictions, by far, is the general fund, at 80.6 percent. This

Table 13. Funding Sources for Economic Development (Percent Reporting)

	All	Cities	Counties	Population <10,000	≥10,000
General fund	80.6	74.7	94.0	67.3	94.4
State grants	39.6	34.7	50.7	34.5	44.9
Federal grants	24.4	24.7	23.9	25.5	23.4
Private funds	18.9	14.0	29.9	9.1	29.0
Hotel tax	13.8	9.3	23.9	6.4	21.5
Sales tax	11.5	13.3	7.5	13.6	9.3
Other	7.4	10.0	1.5	9.1	5.6
Industrial revenue bonds	6.9	2.7	16.4	0.9	13.1
Assessment district	4.1	5.3	1.5	2.7	5.6
Tax increment financing	3.2	1.3	7.5	0.0	6.5
General obligation bonds	2.3	2.7	1.5	2.7	1.9
n	217	150	67	110	107

Table 14. Perspectives on the Role of Local Government in Economic Development (Percent Reporting)

	All	Cities	Counties	Population <10,000	≥10,000
Provide high-quality public services and amenities	35.9	38.7	29.9	40.0	31.8
Provide strategic leadership and facilitation	31.8	29.3	37.3	29.1	34.6
Create a positive business climate	24.9	22.0	31.3	19.1	30.8
Offer incentives to companies when requested	4.6	4.7	4.5	3.6	5.6
n	217	150	67	110	107

Table 15. Perspectives on Governance for Economic Development

	All	Cities	Counties	Population <10,000	≥10,000
Competes with other jurisdictions in region	3.412	3.225	3.806	3.010	3.802
Collaborates with other jurisdictions in region	3.197	2.993	3.627	2.814	3.566
ED organizations have clearly defined roles	3.053	2.899	3.373	2.680	3.406
Adequate citizen input	2.822	2.624	3.239	2.304	3.321
Incentive competition from neighbors	2.892	2.686	3.313	2.459	3.293

Note: Mean score on a 5-point scale

is followed by state grants (39.6 percent), federal grants (24.4 percent), private funds (18.9 percent), hotel taxes (13.8 percent), and sales taxes (11.5 percent). Sixteen percent of counties and 13.1 percent of larger jurisdictions reported using industrial revenue bonds as a funding source, compared to only 2.7 percent of cities and less than 1 percent of smaller communities. Only 4 percent of respondents indicated that they use special assessment districts to fund economic development, though cities (5.3 percent) and larger jurisdictions (5.6 percent) are slightly more likely than counties (1.5 percent) and smaller communities (2.7 percent) to use them. Very few local governments reported using tax increment financing and general obligation bonds to pay for economic development projects.

There is some variation in how respondents view the role of local government in economic development (see Table 14). The highest percentage (35.9 percent) of all responding jurisdictions indicated that the single most important role of local government is to provide high quality services and amenities. This was also true for cities (38.7 percent) and smaller jurisdictions (40.0 percent). By contrast, the highest percentage of counties (37.3 percent) and larger jurisdictions (34.6 percent) perceived that local government's single most important role is to provide strategic leadership and facilitate the process of economic development. This finding supports the premise that counties, in particular, may be inclined to perform a regional coordinating function with respect to economic development.

The survey findings reveal some additional perspectives on governance and service delivery issues. A key question is whether local governments take a mostly competitive posture in relation to nearby jurisdictions, or whether collaboration is the norm in economic development. The results in Table 15 suggest that local governments in North Carolina see them-

selves in competition with other jurisdictions in their respective regions, but that they will also collaborate when necessary. Counties and larger jurisdictions are more likely both to compete and to collaborate with neighboring localities. In addition, counties and larger jurisdictions reported greater role clarity among economic development organizations and showed a stronger tendency for having adequate citizen input on economic development. These respondents also indicated that they are influenced by the incentives provided by other jurisdictions to a greater degree than are cities and smaller communities.

When municipalities and counties collaborate on large scale ventures, such as industrial parks, they can enjoy economies of scale and cost savings and pursue projects that otherwise

Table 16. Participation in Interlocal Agreements (Percent Reporting)

	All	Cities	Counties	Population <10,000	≥10,000
Yes	42.9	39.7	52.2	33.0	54.2
Water and sewer	31.8	27.3	41.8	23.6	40.2
Industrial park	19.4	14.0	31.3	10.0	29.0
Infrastructure improvements	15.2	15.3	14.9	10.0	20.6
Marketing and recruitment	10.6	7.3	17.9	7.3	14.0
Workforce development	6.5	5.3	9.0	3.6	9.3
Transportation	6.0	6.0	6.0	2.7	9.3
Revitalization project	5.1	6.0	3.0	3.6	6.5
Other	4.1	5.3	1.5	1.8	6.5
n	217	150	67	110	107

Table 17. Barriers to Economic Development (Percent Reporting)

	All	Cities	Counties	Population <10,000	≥10,000
Availability of sites and buildings	60.8	53.3	77.6	50.0	72.0
Lack of infrastructure	44.2	36.7	61.2	41.8	46.7
Lack of capital/ funding	42.9	41.3	46.3	42.7	43.0
Limited number of major employers	37.3	37.3	37.3	43.6	30.8
Lack of skilled workforce	27.6	21.3	41.8	17.3	38.3
Inability to retain young people	21.2	20.0	23.9	20.0	22.4
Citizen opposition	17.1	18.7	13.4	20.9	13.1
Lack of leadership	16.6	15.3	19.4	17.3	15.9
Inadequate public schools	16.1	14.7	19.4	11.8	20.6
Lack of recreation and cultural amenities	14.3	14.7	13.4	17.3	11.2
Other	14.3	14.0	14.9	11.8	16.8
Loss of population	12.0	12.7	10.4	16.4	7.5
Lack of political support	11.5	10.0	14.9	10.0	13.1
Lack of regional collaboration	10.6	12.7	6.0	10.9	10.3
n	217	150	67	110	107

might not be feasible. The North Carolina General Assembly has enacted legislation to encourage and facilitate interlocal cooperation on such projects. Section 158-7.4 of the North Carolina General Statutes authorizes two or more units of local government to enter into a contractual agreement to share financing, expenditures, and revenues related to joint development projects. It specifically authorizes the sharing of property tax revenues generated from a joint industrial/commercial park or site. As shown in Table 16, 43 percent of local governments responding to the survey reported having used an interlocal agreement with another jurisdiction in support of economic development. More than half (52.2 percent) of counties had done so, compared to 40 percent of cities. Interlocal agreements are used most frequently for water/sewer projects, industrial parks, infrastructure improvements, and marketing/ business recruitment.

Barriers and Assistance Needs

Understanding what obstacles cities and counties face in their economic development efforts is an important prerequisite for determining how best to provide assistance and enact supportive public policies. The survey results shown in Table 17 suggest that deficiencies in the physical and built environment, limited financial resources, and problems with human resources all hinder the ability of local governments to stimulate private investment. A majority of survey respondents reported that the availability of suitable sites and buildings (or lack thereof) poses a challenge. A majority of counties consider the lack of infrastructure to be problematic. Other barriers reported include a lack of financial capital, too few major employers, and the lack of a skilled workforce. A higher percentage of smaller jurisdictions view citizen opposition as an impediment to economic development.

The local capacity for economic development depends in large part on having access to beneficial information and sources of community assistance. As shown in Table 18, a majority of all responding jurisdictions want information about federal and state funding opportunities. A majority of counties and larger jurisdictions desire to know more about best practices used in other localities. Exactly half of the smaller communities responding to the survey cited a need for information on available technical assistance resources. When asked about specific types of technical assistance needed, survey respondents most often noted strategic planning and grant writing overall (Table 19). The highest percentages of counties and larger jurisdictions seek assistance with estimating the cost and benefits of development.

As shown in Table 20, the local governments responding to the survey tend to rely primarily on two entities for information and assistance with economic development: a regional partnership organization (46.1 percent) and the state Department of Commerce (45.6 percent). Counties and larger jurisdictions are much more likely to contact these organizations for help than are cities and smaller jurisdictions. A higher percentage of smaller jurisdictions reported that a Council of Government (COG) is a source for assistance. Across the board, few respondents appear to utilize local colleges and universities for assistance with economic development.

Table 18. Information Needs for Economic Development (Percent Reporting)

	All	Cities	Counties	Population <10,000	≥10,000
Info. about state and federal grants	56.2	60.0	47.8	63.6	48.6
ED best practices	49.3	46.7	55.2	42.7	56.1
Resources for technical assistance	47.0	46.7	47.8	50.0	43.9
Data for community profile/marketing	35.0	37.3	29.9	38.2	31.8
Other	7.8	4.7	14.9	3.6	12.1
n	217	150	67	110	107

Table 19. Technical Assistance Needs (Percent Reporting)

	All	Cities	Counties	Population <10,000	≥10,000
Strategic planning assistance	40.6	44.7	31.3	48.2	32.7
Grant writing	40.1	41.3	37.3	47.3	32.7
Assessing community assets and opportunities	37.8	42.7	26.9	43.6	31.8
Estimating economic and fiscal impacts	37.3	32.0	49.3	29.1	45.8
Structuring incentive packages	32.7	32.0	34.3	27.3	38.3
Capacity of local ED organizations	23.5	26.0	17.9	21.8	25.2
Other	9.2	6.7	14.9	8.2	10.3
n	217	150	67	110	107

Table 20. Who Do You Turn To for Assistance with Economic Development? (Percent Reporting)

	All	Cities	Counties	Population <10,000	≥10,000
Regional ED partnership	46.1	38.7	62.7	36.4	56.1
State Commerce Department	45.6	37.3	64.2	33.6	57.9
Local gov't staff	34.6	37.3	28.4	36.4	32.7
Chamber of commerce	28.6	32.7	19.4	29.1	28.0
Council of Government	25.8	28.0	20.9	33.6	17.8
Other	16.6	16.0	17.9	14.5	18.7
Local college or university	9.7	8.7	11.9	6.4	13.1
n	217	150	67	110	107

There is no obvious preference among responding local governments for using so-called Type II policies, which encourage a more equitable distribution of economic development benefits. For example, promoting social and economic equity was next to last among reported economic development goals, and a relatively small percentage of jurisdictions impose local hiring requirements on firms receiving incentives. However, a majority of respondents have a formal incentive policy, use cost-benefit analysis, and require incentive performance agreements with clawback provisions. These accountability mechanisms help ensure that economic development incentives serve a broader public purpose that is consistent with the spirit of Type II policies. Their prevalence among local governments in the state may signal a trend that will need to be observed over time.

Local economic development is a function of the resources and capacity for promoting private investment and job creation that are available within a jurisdiction and the external assistance it can tap into.[24] Small communities generally have limitations with respect to both resources and capacity. It is therefore understandable that they might do less to promote economic development. The survey data provide strong support for this proposition. Larger jurisdictions in North Carolina do more to promote economic development across the board. The obvious explanation for this disparity is that smaller towns and counties do less because they have fewer financial, human, and organizational resources. However,

Conclusion and Implications

The survey findings reported here show no evidence of a widespread shift away from traditional industrial recruitment activities in favor of entrepreneurial policies, as suggested by some observers. Business recruitment continues to be the dominant economic development strategy among local governments in North Carolina. Consistent with previous research, the survey findings reveal that local governments in the state rely primarily on infrastructure investments, zoning, and permitting as economic development incentives. Many jurisdictions—counties in particular—also provide cash grants directly to firms in lieu of abating local property taxes, which is prohibited in North Carolina.

---

24. See Edward J. Blakely and Ted K. Bradshaw, Planning Local Economic Development: Theory and Practice, 3rd ed. (Thousand Oaks, CA: Sage Publications, 2002), 55–56. The authors derive the expression: local development = $c \times r$, where c is a community's capacity (economic, social, technological, political) and r represents its resources (natural, human, financial, fiscal, locational, etc.).

the analysis does not capture the extent to which the level of economic development effort might be more related to income and wealth than merely to population size. Since jurisdiction size is likely correlated with economic prosperity, it could be that population size is not as important as the amount of income and wealth within a community.

The premise that smaller jurisdictions are more likely to experiment with nontraditional economic development strategies is not supported by the survey data. The logic here is that smaller communities will turn to alternative strategies that are potentially more effective for them than traditional industrial recruitment activities. The survey results show that smaller jurisdictions do less of everything in economic development, including using alternative strategies such as entrepreneurship development, tourism development, and industry clusters. The lack of support in the survey data for this idea does not negate its underlying logic. It is completely rational for smaller communities to seek suitable alternatives to traditional approaches that have produced mixed results. It could be that smaller jurisdictions are currently at a crossroads. Perhaps they desire and seek new strategies and tools but have not adopted them just yet because of information gaps and uncertainty about what works. It could also be that small communities are too understaffed and constrained to even know what their options are and do not have the requisite capacity to do much of anything without external assistance.

This report examined whether counties play a special role in economic development. More specifically, do counties serve in a regional coordinating capacity on behalf of municipalities? If so, then this regional coordinating role would make them more oriented toward long-term goals, strategic planning, and evaluation and more likely to partner with other entities. The survey findings provide some support for this notion. It was shown that counties embrace a wider range of economic development goals than cities and are more likely to have adopted a formal strategic plan to guide their efforts. Counties also make greater use of various accountability mechanisms, including program evaluation, incentive policies and criteria, performance agreements, and clawback provisions. In addition, counties indicated the strongest tendency to collaborate and involve more organizational partners in administering their economic development programs, and they are more likely to invest in certain quality of life amenities. A potential implication of these findings is that North Carolina counties may indeed be fulfilling a regional coordinating role in economic development. A caveat is that counties may take this broader approach because they have access to greater resources—a possibility not completely accounted for in this analysis.

The survey data showed that counties are more likely than cities to employ nontraditional techniques such as business incubators, export assistance, and workforce development. The survey results showed that counties do in fact use these types of tools and strategies to a greater extent than cities. However, the range of nontraditional techniques used is quite limited. Although they use alternative policies more than cities, counties still seem to prefer traditional business recruitment activities.

Two broad themes emerge from this survey of local government economic development activities in North Carolina. The first has to do with strengthening the capacity to do economic development at the local level. It is clear that small communities are much less engaged in efforts to shape their local economies. Having greater access to information and technical assistance might make a difference among smaller jurisdictions. The survey data also point to a need to provide more systematic support to the local decision-making process regarding economic development, particularly in the areas of strategic planning, best practices, and economic/fiscal impact analysis. In addition, the challenges associated with finding suitable sites and buildings and developing the infrastructure needed to accommodate new private investment will require innovative solutions if substantial financial resources are not forthcoming.

The second overarching theme is about connections. An important part of expanding the local capacity for economic development involves connecting communities to valuable ideas, resources, and opportunities. The connections that matter most are those that spark local innovation, facilitate desired change, produce results, and help a jurisdiction accomplish what it cannot do alone. Counties appear well positioned to be the hub for the economic development activities of smaller municipalities in some instances. In other cases, a multicounty partnership might fulfill that role, but smaller communities must figure out how to ensure that their interests are sufficiently represented in such an arrangement. Whatever the exact form, the potential gains from greater interjurisdictional collaboration on economic development have yet to be fully realized. A missed opportunity revealed in the survey is the low utilization of colleges and universities in local economic development activities. Building stronger connections between institutions of higher education and local economic development programs is a way to both expand capacity at the local level and generate knowledge about the development process.

Appendix

2006 Survey of Local Government
Economic Development Activities in North Carolina

The UNC Institute of Government is conducting this survey of local government economic activities in order to better serve you. Please respond to the following questions on behalf of your jurisdiction or forward to the appropriate person in your unit. You may return your completed questionnaire by mail or fax. The deadline for submitting your responses is **Friday, May 26, 2006.**

General

1. Which of the following statements best describes the entity with <u>primary</u> responsibility for economic development in your jurisdiction? (Check only one.)
   a. ☐ A local government unit has primary responsibility for economic development.
   b. ☐ A nonprofit development organization has primary responsibility for economic development.
   c. ☐ No single organization is primarily responsible for economic development.
   d. ☐ Other (Please describe: _____)

2. Which local government department has <u>primary</u> responsibility for economic development? *(Check only one.)*

   Municipalities (cities and towns)
   a. ☐ City/town manager's office
   b. ☐ Mayor's office
   c. ☐ Planning department
   d. ☐ Economic development department
   e. ☐ Clerk
   f. ☐ Other (specify) _____
   g. ☐ None

   Counties
   a. ☐ County manager's office
   b. ☐ Chair, county commission board
   c. ☐ Planning department
   d. ☐ Economic development department
   e. ☐ Clerk
   f. ☐ Other (specify) _____
   g. ☐ None

3. How would you describe the level of cooperation among your jurisdiction's economic development organizations?
   1. ☐ Very Poor   2. ☐ Poor   3. ☐ Neutral   4. ☐ Good   5. ☐ Very Good

4. A. Which of the following best describes your jurisdiction's current economic base and <u>primary</u> focus of your economic development efforts? *(Check only one in each column.)*

	Current Economic Base	Focus of Economic Development Efforts
a. Agricultural	☐	☐
b. Manufacturing	☐	☐
c. Retail/Service	☐	☐
d. Institutional (government, military, education, etc.)	☐	☐
e. Tourism/Hospitality	☐	☐
f. Residential/"bedroom" community	☐	☐
g. Warehousing/distribution	☐	☐
h. Retirement community	☐	☐
i. High-technology industries	☐	☐
j. Other (specify) _____	☐	☐

B. Which of the above are the top three priorities in your jurisdiction's economic development efforts? *Please write the appropriate letter from the above list in order of priority.*
   1. _____   2. _____   3. _____

2006 Economic Development Survey

5. Which of the following best describes the condition of your jurisdiction's economic base (1) during the last five years and (2) which do you think it will be over the next five years? *(Check only __one__ in each column.)*

		Last 5 Years	Next 5 Years
a.	Rapid expansion (more than 25%)	☐	☐
b.	Moderate growth (10-25%)	☐	☐
c.	Slow growth (less than 10%)	☐	☐
d.	Stable – No growth or decline	☐	☐
e.	Slow decline (less than 10%)	☐	☐
f.	Moderate decline (10-25%)	☐	☐
g.	Rapid decline (more than 25%)	☐	☐

6. Please approximate the percentage of time and resources your jurisdiction devotes to each of the following economic development activities (percentages should total 100%).

   a. Business recruitment _____%   b. Business retention _____%   c. Small business creation _____%

Planning and Evaluation

7. A. Does your local government have a written strategic plan for economic development?

   a. ☐ Yes   b. ☐ No

   B. If YES, who prepared the plan?

   a. ☐ In-house staff
   b. ☐ University faculty
   c. ☐ Private consultant
   d. ☐ Council of Govt./Regional Partnership
   e. ☐ Other (specify) _____

   C. When was the plan prepared or last updated?

   a. ☐ Within the last year
   b. ☐ 1-2 years ago
   c. ☐ 3-5 years ago
   d. ☐ 6-10 years ago
   e. ☐ Over 10 years ago

8. A. What are your jurisdiction's economic development goals? (Check all that apply.)

   a. ☐ Job creation
   b. ☐ Higher paying/better jobs
   c. ☐ Expand the tax base
   d. ☐ Diversify the economic base
   e. ☐ Retain and expand existing businesses
   f. ☐ Recruit new businesses
   g. ☐ Attract retail and services not currently available
   h. ☐ Promote entrepreneurship and small business
   i. ☐ Control growth/smart growth
   j. ☐ Promote social and economic equity
   k. ☐ Wealth creation
   l. ☐ Other (specify) _____

   B. Which of the above goals are most important? *Please give the appropriate letter from the above list in order of priority.*

   1. _____   2. _____   3. _____

9. Does your local government systematically evaluate its economic development activities?

   a. ☐ Yes   b. ☐ No

10. If YES, how do you measure the success of your economic development efforts? (Check all that apply.)

   a. ☐ Input measures (e.g., number of staff hours expended)
   b. ☐ Output measures (e.g., number of companies served)
   c. ☐ Efficiency measures (e.g., program expenditures per estimated tax revenue generated)
   d. ☐ Outcome measures (e.g., number of jobs created, amount of capital investment)
   e. ☐ Other (Please specify.) _____

Business Recruitment

11. A. Which of the following does your local government use to recruit <u>new</u> business? (Check all that apply.)

a. ☐ Promotional and advertising activities
b. ☐ Local govt. staff calls on business prospects
c. ☐ Responding to inquiries from prospects
d. ☐ Cluster targeting of specific industries
e. ☐ Cash grant incentive payments
f. ☐ Hosting site visits
g. ☐ Attendance at conferences/trade shows
h. ☐ Website/community profile

i. ☐ Building and sites inventory
j. ☐ Partnership with chamber of commerce
k. ☐ Collaboration with regional econ. dev. partnership
l. ☐ Worker training assistance
m. ☐ Provide high quality of life
n. ☐ State-sponsored trade missions abroad
o. ☐ Other (specify) _____
p. ☐ No recruitment activities by local government

B. Which of the above recruitment methods does your local government utilize the most? *Please write the appropriate letter from the above list in order of priority.*
   1._____   2._____

Business Retention and Expansion

12. A. Which of the following does your local government use to retain and support <u>existing</u> businesses? (Check all that apply.)

a. ☐ Local govt. representative calls on existing industry
b. ☐ Cash grant incentive payments
c. ☐ Surveys of local businesses
d. ☐ Local business publicity program
e. ☐ Business achievement/recognition awards
f. ☐ Partnering with other local governments
g. ☐ Business networking activities
h. ☐ Revolving loan fund

i. ☐ Business ombudsman program
j. ☐ Worker training assistance
k. ☐ Replacing imports with local goods
l. ☐ Export development assistance
m. ☐ Partnering with non-governmental entities
n. ☐ Industry cluster program
o. ☐ Other (specify) _____
p. ☐ No retention activities by local government

B. Which of the above retention methods does your local government utilize the most? *Please write the appropriate letter from the above list in order of priority.*
   1._____   2._____

Small Business Creation and Entrepreneurship

13. A. Which of the following methods does your local government use to help create and grow small businesses? (Check all that apply.)

a. ☐ Revolving loan fund
b. ☐ Small business development center
c. ☐ Matching grants to upgrade business properties
d. ☐ Business incubator
e. ☐ Microenterprise program
f. ☐ Equity/venture capital financing

g. ☐ Marketing assistance
h. ☐ Executive on loan/mentoring
i. ☐ Management training
j. ☐ Vendor/supplier matching
k. ☐ Other (specify) _____
l. ☐ No small business activities by local government

B. Which of the above small business development methods does your local government utilize the most? *Please write the appropriate letter from the above list in order of priority.*
   1._____   2._____

2006 Economic Development Survey

Quality of Life

14. A. Which of the following does your local government invest in as <u>part of its economic development efforts</u>? (Check all that apply.)

a. ☐ Tourism development
b. ☐ Convention center
c. ☐ Theater or arts center
d. ☐ Professional sports arena
e. ☐ Downtown development
f. ☐ Development of local arts
g. ☐ Child care
h. ☐ Local libraries

i. ☐ Affordable housing
j. ☐ Amateur sports/recreation complex
k. ☐ Medical/health care facilities
l. ☐ Local school system/public education
m. ☐ Historic preservation
n. ☐ Public parks
o. ☐ Transportation and mass transit
p. ☐ Public safety

Incentives

15. A. Which of the following business incentives does your local government offer? (Check all that apply.)

a. ☐ Zoning/permit assistance
b. ☐ Infrastructure improvements
c. ☐ One-stop permitting
d. ☐ Land or building acquisition
e. ☐ Cash grant incentive payments
f. ☐ Local tax credits
g. ☐ Regulatory flexibility
h. ☐ Employee screening
i. ☐ Site preparation

j. ☐ Incentives for retail projects
k. ☐ Subsidized worker training
l. ☐ Private utility rate reduction
m. ☐ State development zone designation
n. ☐ Subsidized land or buildings
o. ☐ Low-interest loans
p. ☐ Relocation assistance
q. ☐ Tax increment /project development financing
r. ☐ Other (specify) _____

B. Which of the above incentives does your local government utilize the most? *Please write the appropriate letter from the above list in order of priority.*

1._____   2. _____

C. How does your jurisdiction use the incentives you selected above in its economic development efforts? (Check only one.)

a. ☐ Mostly to recruit <u>new</u> industry
b. ☐ Balanced between recruiting new companies and retaining existing industry
c. ☐ Mostly to retain and support <u>existing</u> industry

16. A. Do you always require a written performance agreement as a condition for providing business incentives?

a. ☐ Always   b. ☐ Sometimes   c. ☐ Never

B. Does your jurisdiction perform a cost/benefit analysis prior to offering business incentives?   ☐Yes   ☐No
C. Does your jurisdiction have a formal policy for determining eligibility for business incentives?   ☐Yes   ☐No
D. Does your local government ever require a percentage of new employees to be hired locally?   ☐Yes   ☐No
E. Do you require companies to return/repay incentives if they fail to meet performance targets?   ☐Yes   ☐No

F. Please indicate any change in dollar value of the average business incentive package over the last five years? (Check the appropriate number.)

1.☐ Much less   2.☐ Slightly less   3.☐ About the same   4.☐ Slightly larger   5.☐ Much larger

17. Which of the following criteria are your local incentives based on? (Check all that apply.)
    a. ☐ Number of new jobs created
    b. ☐ Amount of investment in land, building, and equipment
    c. ☐ Company performance (revenue, sales, etc.)
    d. ☐ Type of business/industry
    e. ☐ Wage levels of new jobs
    f. ☐ Public investment payback period
    g. ☐ New tax revenue generated
    h. ☐ Other (specify) _____

Service Delivery

18. What is the level of your local government's participation in the following economic development activities?

	Very Low		Moderate		Very High
a. Construction and marketing of shell buildings	1	2	3	4	5
b. Land banking and assembly	1	2	3	4	5
c. Industrial parks owned/operated by local government	1	2	3	4	5
d. Local government-sponsored loan programs	1	2	3	4	5
e. Equity financing for private companies	1	2	3	4	5
f. Workforce development/job training	1	2	3	4	5
g. Community development corporation	1	2	3	4	5

19. A. Which of the following participate in your jurisdiction's economic development efforts? (Check all that apply.)
    a. ☐ Municipal government
    b. ☐ County government
    c. ☐ Chamber of commerce
    d. ☐ Citizen advisory board
    e. ☐ Community development corporation
    f. ☐ Private utility company
    g. ☐ Local economic development commission
    h. ☐ Industrial development authority
    i. ☐ Local community college
    j. ☐ Nonprofit economic development corporation
    k. ☐ Elected officials
    l. ☐ Federal government
    m. ☐ State Department of Commerce
    n. ☐ Regional economic development partnership
    o. ☐ Council of Government (COG)
    p. ☐ Local workforce investment board
    q. ☐ University
    r. ☐ Other (specify) _____

    B. Which two of the above groups are most involved in economic development in your jurisdiction? *Please write the appropriate letter from the above list in order of priority.*
        1._____   2. _____

Barriers to Economic Development

20. A. Which of the following barriers to economic development has your local government encountered? (Check all that apply.)
    a. ☐ Citizen opposition
    b. ☐ Availability of sites and buildings
    c. ☐ Lack of regional collaboration
    d. ☐ Lack of skilled workforce
    e. ☐ Lack of infrastructure
    f. ☐ Loss of population
    g. ☐ Lack of leadership
    h. ☐ Lack of capital/funding
    i. ☐ Lack of political support
    j. ☐ Inadequate public school system
    k. ☐ Lack of recreation and cultural amenities
    l. ☐ Inability to retain young people
    m. ☐ Limited number of major employers
    n. ☐ Other (specify) _____

    B. Please indicate the top two barriers to economic development by putting the corresponding letter in the space provided (in order of priority).   1._____   2._____

2006 Economic Development Survey

Expanding Local Capacity

21. What types of information does your local government need to strengthen its economic development efforts? (Check all that apply.)
    a. ☐ Information about state and federal grant/funding opportunities
    b. ☐ Information about economic development best practices used in other jurisdictions
    c. ☐ Information about available resources for economic development technical assistance
    d. ☐ Economic and demographic data to create community profile for marketing
    e. ☐ Other (specify) _____
    f. ☐ None

22. Who are you most likely to contact when you need information or have a question about economic development? (Check all that apply.)
    a. ☐ Local government staff
    b. ☐ Local college or university
    c. ☐ Local chamber of commerce
    d. ☐ Regional Economic Development partnership organization
    e. ☐ Council of Government
    f. ☐ State Commerce Department
    g. ☐ Other (specify) _____

23. What types of technical assistance does your jurisdiction need to improve its economic development capabilities? (Check all that apply.)
    a. ☐ Strategic planning assistance
    b. ☐ Grant writing
    c. ☐ Assistance in assessing community assets and opportunities for economic development
    d. ☐ Assistance in improving the capacity of local economic development organizations
    e. ☐ Structuring incentive packages
    f. ☐ Estimating the economic and fiscal impacts of development
    g. ☐ Other (specify) _____

24. Would you support a program offering economic development training courses for local officials? ☐ Yes ☐ No

    A. If YES, which of the following topics would be most beneficial? (Check all that apply.).
    a. ☐ Business recruitment
    b. ☐ Commercial/retail development
    c. ☐ Business retention and expansion
    d. ☐ Tourism/retiree attraction
    e. ☐ Organizing for economic development
    f. ☐ Real estate development
    g. ☐ Economic development finance
    h. ☐ Marketing strategies
    i. ☐ Small business/entrepreneurship dev.
    j. ☐ Tax increment/project development financing
    k. ☐ Economic/fiscal impact analysis
    l. ☐ Incentives as a public investment
    m. ☐ Strategic planning for economic development
    n. ☐ Grant writing and fundraising
    o. ☐ Building community involvement
    p. ☐ Rural development strategies
    q. ☐ Overview of economic development strategies
    r. ☐ Environmental issues
    s. ☐ Economic development training for elected officials
    t. ☐ Leadership development
    u. ☐ Evaluating economic development programs
    v. ☐ Regional tax base/revenue sharing
    w. ☐ Growth management
    x. ☐ Other (specify) _____

B. From the above list, please indicate the top two most important training topics needed in your jurisdiction by writing the corresponding letters in the spaces provided (in order of priority). 1. _____   2. _____

C. Who in your jurisdiction do you think would benefit the most from such an economic development training program? (Select only one.)

    a. ☐ Local government staff/administrators

    b. ☐ Elected officials

    c. ☐ Appointed boards and commissions

Economic Development Perspectives

25. What is the single most important role for local government in the process of economic development? *(Check only one.)*

    a. ☐ Create a positive business climate (low taxes, streamline regulations, etc.)

    b. ☐ Provide high quality public services and amenities (schools, infrastructure, etc.)

    c. ☐ Offer incentives to companies when requested

    d. ☐ Provide strategic leadership and proactively facilitate the process

    e. ☐ Other (specify) _____

26. Please indicate your level of agreement with the following statements by circling the number that best corresponds to your viewpoint.

	Strongly Disagree				Strongly Agree
a. Our jurisdiction competes with other jurisdictions in the region for economic development.	1	2	3	4	5
b. Our jurisdiction collaborates with other jurisdictions in the region on economic development.	1	2	3	4	5
c. The roles of the various economic development organizations serving this jurisdiction are clearly defined.	1	2	3	4	5
d. There is adequate citizen input into our economic development activities.	1	2	3	4	5
e. The incentives offered by other jurisdictions strongly influence the types of incentives we provide.	1	2	3	4	5

27. A. Has your local government ever entered into a formal interlocal agreement with another jurisdiction to do a joint economic development project?   ☐ Yes ☐ No

    B. If so, on what types of economic development projects? (Check all that apply.)

    a. ☐ Water/sewer   e. ☐ Development/revitalization project

    b. ☐ Infrastructure improvement   f. ☐ Workforce development/job training

    c. ☐ Industrial park   g. ☐ Marketing/recruitment

    d. ☐ Transportation   h. ☐ Other (specify) _____

28. A. Please identify who your jurisdiction competes with in attracting private investment. (Check all that apply.)

    a. ☐ Nearby local governments in the region   d. ☐ Other state governments

    b. ☐ Other local governments in the state   e. ☐ Foreign countries

    c. ☐ Local governments in surrounding states   f. ☐ Other (specify) _____

2006 Economic Development Survey

B. Please indicate the top competitor from above by putting the corresponding letter in the space provided.
1._____

Local Government/Jurisdiction Profile

29. Name _____

30. Title _____

31. Name of Jurisdiction _____

32. County_____

33. What is the total operating budget for your jurisdiction in FY 2005-2006? _____

34. How would you characterize your jurisdiction's tax base? (Check only one.)
☐ Mostly residential   ☐ mostly retail/commercial   ☐ mostly industrial   ☐ diverse mix of all three

35. How many of your local government's professional staff spends at least 75% of their time on economic development? _____

36. How much did your jurisdiction budget for Economic Development in FY 2005-06? _____
A. List the top two funded activities. 1. _____ 2. _____

B. Roughly what percent of the total budget for economic development was funded by: (should total 100%)
1. Local government _____%   2. Private sector _____%   3. Other_____% *please specify* _____

C. Do you think your economic development budget over the next five years will:

Significantly Decrease   **Remain the same**   **Significantly Increase**
1☐   2☐   3☐   4☐   5☐

37. Please indicate which of the following sources are used to fund your economic development activities. (Check all that apply.)
a. ☐ Local revenues/general fund   g. ☐ General obligation bonds
b. ☐ Special assessment districts   h. ☐ Industrial revenue bonds
c. ☐ Federal grants   i. ☐ Tax increment/project development financing
d. ☐ State grants   j. ☐ Hotel/motel taxes
e. ☐ Private funds   k. ☐ Other (specify) _____
f. ☐ Sales tax

38. Does your jurisdiction have a web site on the Internet for economic development purposes? ☐Yes ☐No

39. Please share contact information for an innovative economic development project in your jurisdiction that you think others in the state might benefit from learning about: _____
_____

Thank you for completing the economic development survey!
Please return the completed survey using the enclosed self-addressed, postage paid envelope to:
Dr. Jonathan Morgan, Institute of Government, UNC-Chapel Hill, CB# 3330, Chapel Hill, NC 27599-3330.
or fax to: 919-962-0654

www.ingramcontent.com/pod-product-compliance
Lightning Source LLC
Chambersburg PA
CBHW080621270326
41928CB00016B/3151

*9 7 8 1 5 6 0 1 1 6 1 2 7 *